Waltham Forest Libraries

Please return this item by the last date stamped. The loan may be renewed unless required by another customer.

12/2021		

D1493641

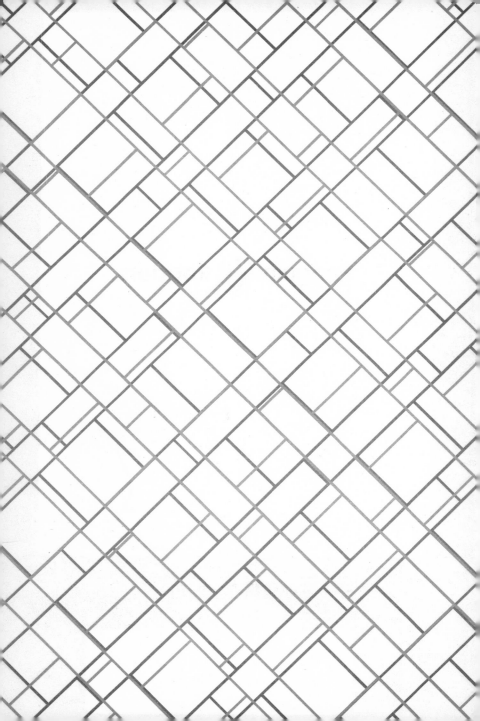

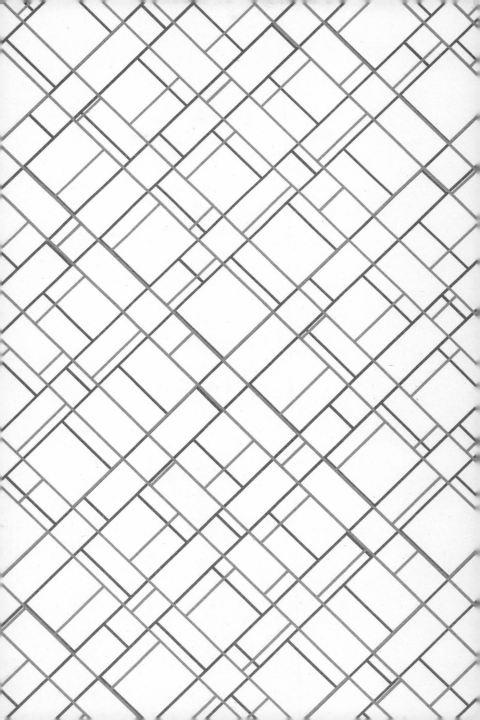

FRANKENSTEIN

MARY SHELLEY

LEVEL

5

RETOLD BY HELEN HOLWILL
ILLUSTRATED BY ROHAN EASON
SERIES EDITOR: SORREL PITTS

PENGUIN BOOKS

UK | USA | Canada | Ireland | Australia
India | New Zealand | South Africa

Penguin Books is part of the Penguin Random House group of companies
whose addresses can be found at global.penguinrandomhouse.com.
www.penguin.co.uk www.puffin.co.uk www.ladybird.co.uk

Penguin Readers edition of *Frankenstein* published by Penguin Books Ltd, 2020
001

Original text written by Mary Shelley
Text for Penguin Readers edition adapted by Helen Holwill
Text for Penguin Readers edition copyright © Penguin Books Ltd, 2020
Inside illustrated by Rohan Eason
Illustrations copyright © Rohan Eason, 2020

Printed and bound in Great Britain by Clays Ltd, Elcograf S.p.A.

A CIP catalogue record for this book is available from the British Library

ISBN: 978–0–241–43094–1

All correspondence to
Penguin Books
Penguin Random House Children's
One Embassy Gardens, New Union Square
5 Nine Elms Lane, London SW8 5DA

MIX
Paper from
responsible sources
FSC® C018179

Penguin Random House is committed to a
sustainable future for our business, our readers
and our planet. This book is made from Forest
Stewardship Council® certified paper.

Contents

Note about the story

Mary Shelley (1797–1851) was an English writer who is well known for her book *Frankenstein*. Her mother died soon after she was born, and she had a very difficult life. In 1814, she fell in love with a famous English writer called Percy Shelley. They had four children, but three of their children died while they were still babies.

Mary and Percy travelled around Europe together and shared a love of reading, writing and art. In the summer of 1816, they went on holiday to Lake Geneva, Switzerland, with a group of friends. The weather was very bad, and to pass the time the group decided to have a writing competition. It was during this holiday that Mary wrote what later became the book *Frankenstein*. It tells the story of a young **scientist*** who decides to try to make a person and **create** life.

*Definitions of words in **bold** can be found in the glossary on pages 91–93.

Before-reading questions

1 Look at the cover of the book. Have you heard of the story of Frankenstein? What do you think the story is going to be about?

2 What do the words "monster" and "creature" mean? Use the definitions on pages 91 and 92 to help you. What is the difference between these words?

3 Read the "Note about the story". During the time Mary Shelley lived, it was not unusual for people to die very young. Why do you think this was? How do you think Mary Shelley saw life and death?

4 Read the back cover of the book. Are these sentences true or false? Write your answers in your notebook.

   a Frankenstein is a creature made from pieces of bodies.

   b Victor Frankenstein is lonely and angry after he completes the creature.

   c The creature wants to kill Victor Frankenstein.

5 The story was written at the time when electricity was first discovered. Find out about Benjamin Franklin and his famous experiment with electricity. How do you think people felt about the fast-changing world of science at this time?

6 Look at this picture from the story. What is happening? Who do you think this man is? What might he be thinking and feeling?

CHAPTER ONE
A journey to the North Pole

In which Robert Walton writes letters to his sister . . .

28th March 1797, Archangel, Russia

To Mrs Saville, England

My dear sister,

I am now in the far north of Russia, waiting to start my long and difficult journey to the North Pole. I am so full of excitement. I will be the first person to go to a place where no human has ever walked before! I know that you were not happy when I decided to come here, but I hope you understand that my journey has an important purpose. I aim to discover a way for ships to pass near the North Pole and go safely from the Atlantic Ocean through the ice to the Pacific Ocean. Oh, if I achieved that, I would make a wonderful difference to the world!

*After all the years of planning and hard work, I am now ready. I have found a good ship here, and I have paid some **sailors** to come with me. They are all brave and able men, although I do not think any of them will become my friends. We will start our adventure very soon! If I succeed, many, many months will pass before you and I meet again. If I fail, then you will either see me again soon, or never. Goodbye, my dear, kind Margaret!*

Your loving brother,
Robert Walton

7th July 1797, the Arctic Ocean

My dear sister,

I am writing a few sentences to tell you that I am safe.
There is a ship that is now returning home from the north, and I shall
give this letter to one of its sailors to carry.

The journey is going well. It is awfully cold here, and we are
beginning to see more areas of ice, but my men seem happy and work
well together. Although I am well, I feel very alone on this ship. I miss
having a friend — someone who is like me, and with whom I could talk.

Well, I must finish now. Please do not worry about me!

Yours,
R. W.

5th August 1797, the Arctic Ocean

Dear sister,

Something very strange has happened, and I want to write everything down.

Six days ago we came to a place where there was flat, white ice everywhere around us. It was very dangerous because it was also foggy, and we could not easily move. When the fog slowly began to lift, we saw the strangest thing about half a mile from the ship. It was a **sledge** that was moving quickly towards the north. Dogs were pulling it along, and sitting on it was the huge shape of a man, who was much bigger than any human I have ever seen. Moments later, the sledge disappeared into the fog.

The next day, the fog had gone, and we were able to move forward again. But, as the men were getting everything ready, I heard them shout and saw them looking out to sea. Near the ship was a large piece of ice, and on it was a sledge very like the one we had seen the day before. The dogs that had pulled it were all dead, but on the sledge was a man who was still alive. He was extremely cold, so we immediately brought him on to the ship. I have never seen a man so tired, thin and ill.

We carefully looked after him for two days – we kept him warm and gave him small amounts of soup.

He was nothing like the person we had seen on the other sledge. He was a European, and the few words he managed to say were spoken in very good English.

"Where is the ship going?" he asked.

"We are going to the North Pole," I replied.

"Good. I am following someone, and I must continue my search."

"If the man you are looking for is also travelling by sledge, then I think we have seen him," I told him. "The day before we found you, we saw him and his dogs moving towards the north."

"Yes! That must be him!" he told me, and then he asked many questions about what we had seen. Since arriving on the ship, he has seemed **upset** and worried. He is getting stronger each day, but he has not said any more about the other man. I will continue my writing when there is more news to share.

13th August

I am happy to say that the new gentleman on our ship is feeling much better. He now spends all day looking out across the ice, trying to find the man he is searching for.

We have talked a lot, and I have discovered that he is extremely intelligent and interesting. Do you remember my last letter, dear sister? In which I said that I felt alone on this ship? Well, I do believe that this clever, brave stranger is becoming my friend. I like him very much, but I still know very little about him, and he seems so terribly, terribly sad. I told him about my plan to discover a way through to the Pacific Ocean and how dangerous it is. I explained that I would give everything – my money, my family, my life – in order to achieve my aim! It was very strange – at that moment he became very upset and started to cry.

"Oh! Don't say that!" he said, shaking his head. "I used to say the same things. Like you, I had big dreams, and big **discoveries** to make. And now I am full of **regret** – I have lost everything, and my *life is finished. But you have hope, and a good future ahead of you. If you knew my story, you would never again speak like this!"*

I told him that I wanted to help him.

"Nobody can help me now," he replied, quietly. "There is still one thing I must do, and then I will be able to die. If you listen to my story, you will understand."

I am shocked, and of course I want to know more. We agreed that he will start to tell me his full story tomorrow. I promise that I will write every word of it here on these pages, for you to read.

CHAPTER TWO
Victor's early years

In which Victor Frankenstein tells his story . . .

My name is Victor Frankenstein, and I am from Geneva in Switzerland. My story begins many years ago when my father, Alphonse, who came from a very good family, met and married a beautiful and kind young woman called Caroline. After a time, I was born, and we became a happy little family.

My mother wanted to have a daughter, but that did not happen, and for several years I was their only child. Then, when I was about five years old, my mother heard of a poor girl whose parents had both died. She was a little younger than I was, and she was extremely pretty, with blue eyes and hair the colour of gold.

My parents were told that she had come from a very important family in Milan but now had no family and no home. Soon, it was decided that Elizabeth Lavenza would come and live with us as part of our family. Elizabeth was wonderful, and everyone loved her. We spent our early years laughing, playing and learning together. I called her my cousin, but she was much more than that to me.

There were other people who were also important to me when I was a child. We had a young maid called Justine, who lived in our house and helped to look after us.

She was kind, and I really liked her. Then, when I was seven, my parents had another baby − a sweet boy called William. Later, I had to go to school, but I met a boy called Henry Clerval, and we became very close friends. Oh! Back in those days when I was a child, I was very, very happy. Why did those days have to end?

As I grew, I became interested in science, which of course was a new and exciting thing to me. I read many books on the subject and wanted to explore how the world worked. Then, one evening, when I was about fifteen years old, there was a terrible thunderstorm. The thunder was very loud and frightening, and I stood at the door and watched the storm as it came from the mountains and towards our house. Then, suddenly, a big old tree that was very near our house became a huge, very bright wall of fire. I stood and stared. As soon as the bright light disappeared, I saw that the tree had completely gone!

A **professor** of science who was a family friend was staying with us at that time. He explained to me that the fire I had seen was **lightning** and was made of something called **electricity**. Although I had read many books, I had not yet learned about electricity. I was amazed, and I really needed to know more. It was on that dark, stormy night that I decided my future. I definitely wanted to become a **scientist** and make big discoveries.

When I reached the age of seventeen, my parents decided that I should study science at Ingolstadt University.

But, several weeks before the date when I would leave home, Elizabeth became very ill. She had a terrible fever, and she was in a lot of danger. My wonderful mother stayed by the side of her bed and cared for her day and night. Elizabeth was saved, but I am very sorry to say that my mother then became very ill herself, and she was not as lucky as Elizabeth. I will never forget her last words. She joined the hands of Elizabeth and myself and said, "My children, I have always thought that in the future you should marry. You are right for each other, and it will make your father very happy. And you mustn't worry about me – I have had a full and happy life."

Death is an awful thing, and that was the first time I had seen it. But I need not describe how I felt at that time. I am sure you know what it is like, or can imagine.

We were all shocked and upset, but life had to continue, and my father wanted me to go to university as we had planned. Soon the day came, and with difficulty I said goodbye to my father, my brother, William, my dear Elizabeth and my very good friend Henry Clerval.

CHAPTER THREE
Ingolstadt University

It was a long and tiring journey to Ingolstadt, and when I arrived I felt a little alone and nervous. When I met some of the professors who were going to teach me, I quickly realized how little I knew. But I was excited by how much I would surely learn. In the first few weeks I found one professor much more interesting than the others. His name was Professor Waldman, and he was a short man of about fifty years of age. I was amazed by the things he described. He explained how blood moves around the human body, and how the air we breathe keeps us alive. He told us about new and exciting discoveries, and the many wonders of modern science. Then he showed us special machines and other **scientific** objects in his interesting **laboratory.**

As I listened to this scientist, I became more and more sure that I wanted to **create** new things. I wanted to be famous, and I would show the whole world the secrets of **creation**! From that day forward, I thought only about science. I went to every class, and I spent my days studying books and working in the laboratory. Then I made my own laboratory in my apartment so that I could study and do my own **experiments** at any time, day or night.

Two full years passed in this way. My studies took all of my time, and I did not once return home to visit my family. Of course, because of these many hours of study, I learned a huge amount, and the professors were very pleased with my work.

There was now one area of science that really interested me – the human body, or any animal that had life. I had a lot of questions I wanted to answer. What does it mean to be "alive"? Where does life come from? And could man ever create life through science? Could electricity help to create life? But to study life fully, a scientist must also study and understand death. So I began to carefully study dead human bodies. I worked alone, and often all night. I learned about all the different body parts, but I also watched how bodies slowly change after death. The more I saw, the more I became interested in the moment when life appears, and the moment when it leaves. And then one day something amazing happened. Little by little I had become the first person to really understand the creation of life!

I can see by the way you are looking at me, my friend, that you want me to tell you the secret of life. But I cannot tell you. Listen carefully to the rest of my story, and then you will understand why it must always be secret. It is dangerous to know too much. A man who believes that his home town is the complete world is a happy man. He is happier than a man who is always trying to become greater than he should be. And now I shall return to my story.

When I made the discovery, I immediately realized the importance of the **power** I held in my hands. I thought for a long time before I did anything with that information.

I knew how to give life, but to what was I going to give that life? I thought about using something small – an animal perhaps. But no, I decided that I should be brave and aim to create a man. The work would take a very long time and be very difficult, and I knew I would make mistakes and have many problems. But making a man was now my dream, and I wanted to achieve it.

I believed that a small person would be more difficult to make, so I planned to create a huge man, almost eight feet tall. I spent months finding everything I needed, and then I began my work. I worked late into the night, and by the light of the moon I searched the town for dead bodies to use. I brought the bones and body parts back to the laboratory in my apartment, where I worked on them, often doing experiments all day and night.

The summer came and went, but I did not see any of it. The only thing I could think about was finishing this important and difficult job. I became very tired and thin, and I never saw anyone. During all these months I kept my horrible creation secret. Sometimes what I saw in front of me made me nervous about what I was doing. But I knew that I had the information to create life, and I was excited about that. I had to at least try it!

CHAPTER FOUR
Victor's creation

It was on a dark, wet night in November that I finished the work that had taken me almost two years. I was extremely nervous as I began to give life to the completed thing that lay in front of me. It was 1 a.m., and the rain was falling heavily against the window, when I saw the **creature's** yellow, watery eye open for the first time. It breathed hard, and its arms and legs suddenly jumped a little on the table where it lay.

How can I describe what I felt in that terrible moment? I had chosen every part of him carefully – from his straight, white teeth to his long, strong legs. I had wanted him to be as handsome as possible. Handsome! How stupid I had been! In life, he was horrible. His yellow skin and his strange face were ugly and frightened me. I ran out of the laboratory and into my bedroom, where I walked up and down for a long time because I was unable to sleep.

After several hours I lay on the bed and tried to sleep, but then I had a **nightmare**. At first I thought I saw Elizabeth, and she looked beautiful and happy. Then, as I moved towards her to hold her in my arms, her face began to change. Her skin became very white, and then I did not see Elizabeth but my dead mother in my arms! Oh! What a terrible dream! I woke from my sleep with the shock of it.

I then sat up and saw, by the light of the moon, the horrible **monster** I had created. He was standing by the bed and was looking straight at me. His mouth opened and some sounds came out, and next I saw a horrible smile on his face. I was very frightened. Then, as he slowly reached out one arm towards me, I jumped out of bed and ran downstairs. After that, I passed an awful night hiding in the garden.

The next morning, I walked the streets of Ingolstadt because I was too afraid to return to the apartment. It was raining, but I did not care – I walked for miles. While I was walking, I passed the **inn** where many travellers stopped when they came to Ingolstadt. I saw a **carriage** slow down and stop in the road in front of me, and out climbed my good friend Henry Clerval! I was very happy to see him. He told me that he, too, had now come to Ingolstadt to study at the university. I asked him about my father, brother and Elizabeth.

"They are well," he told me. "But they are not very happy that you never write or visit them." He then stopped and looked straight at me.

"My dear Frankenstein, you look terribly ill! You are very thin, and your face is white."

Although I was very nervous, I invited Clerval to come to my apartment. When we arrived there, I asked him to wait downstairs while I went up first. I was frightened, but, when I looked around the place, the creature had gone! Oh! How wonderful! I ran downstairs and asked Clerval to come up with me. We had breakfast together and talked and talked. It was very good to have Clerval with me, but I decided that I could tell him nothing about what I had done. Then, suddenly, while we were talking, I thought I saw the monster in the apartment behind Clerval. Of course, the creature was not really there, but I was nervous and **scared** and was imagining things. I screamed, "It's him! Oh! Save me, save me!" and then I **fainted** on to the floor. I felt very ill. I was so upset and shocked by what had happened that I think I was beginning to see things that weren't really there.

For several months I lay in my bed while my dear friend Clerval looked after me. He saved me. It was not until the spring that I felt better, and he gave me a letter that had arrived from Elizabeth several days before.

To my dear Victor,

I've been very worried about you. Henry tells me that you are a little better now, and he hopes that you will soon be able to write to me.

Your father is well, but he misses you, and William is growing taller every day, but he is still a very sweet boy! There is a lot for me to do here, but Justine is still with us and has been a big help to me in the house. Please write to us, my dear Victor!

Yours,
Elizabeth Lavenza

I wrote a reply to Elizabeth immediately, but it was many weeks until I started to get much better. I still felt weak, and I had no interest at all in science. Henry knew that I had experienced something terrible, but he was careful not to ask me any questions. I was pleased because I did not want to talk about the awful thing I had done.

It was the following spring before I felt well again. Clerval and I spent two weeks walking in the beautiful mountains, and, at last, I felt happy and free again.

CHAPTER FIVE
Bad news

When Clerval and I returned from our walking holiday, there was a letter from my father waiting for me.

My dear Victor,

*I know that you will soon be coming home to us, and that it should be a wonderful, happy time. But I **regret** that I have some awful news. There is no easy way to say it. Your dear, sweet brother, William, has been murdered! Last Thursday it was a beautiful evening, and Elizabeth, William and I went for a long walk. On the walk, William was running and hiding in the trees, but then he didn't return. We looked everywhere for him, again and again, but we couldn't find him. It was at about 5 a.m. that I found my dear boy, dead on the grass! The black marks of the murderer's fingers were around his neck. When Elizabeth saw this she fell down ill, saying, "Oh no! I have done this to him! I allowed him to wear the expensive necklace with a picture of his mother on it, and it has gone! The murderer has taken it!"*

We do not know who the killer is, and I do not want to be full of hate for that person. Please come home to us so that we can be together.

Your loving, sad father,
Alphonse Frankenstein

The very next day I started the long journey back to my home city of Geneva, where I had not been for nearly six years. I was full of sadness during the journey, but there was also some happiness because I was going home. It was dark by the time I got down from the carriage and started to walk the last few miles to our house. As I walked the weather changed, and a loud thunderstorm came. I watched the lightning coming down from the dark sky to the hills, and I felt the rain on my skin. The weather seemed right for my arrival, and right for the terrible thoughts that were in my **mind** about William's death.

Then, moments later, the shape of a huge person came out of the darkness. A sudden **flash** of lightning lit the sky, and I saw the face – it was the face of the monster! But why was he here? Could he be the murderer of my brother? I felt sure that he was. Then, as quickly as he had appeared, he was gone again. With the next flash of light I could see that he was quite far away, and he was beginning to climb up the nearest mountain.

I was terribly shocked. The rain stopped, and I spent the rest of the night outside.

I was cold and wet, but I did not care. I was full of regret, and all I could think about was my awful creation. What had I done? This dangerous monster had gone out into the world and killed someone!

When it got light, I went on walking and arrived at the house early in the morning. Oh! How happy and yet sad I was to see my father. After talking for a few moments, he told me the latest news. "The murderer has now been discovered."

I did not understand, because I had just seen the monster running free. "But who is it?" I asked.

I saw sadness in my father's face as he spoke. "It's . . . Justine."

"Justine!" I cried. "How can that be true?"

"I'm afraid it is."

"No!" I replied. "You are wrong. It can't be Justine!"

"She is guilty. It must be her – she was out all night when it happened, and then we found the necklace that William had around his neck in her pocket."

Justine was in real danger, but what could I do? I knew no one would believe the story of how I created the monster. They would surely think I was mad, so I said nothing more. Three days later, Justine was **hanged**. That kind, beautiful young woman was dead! Oh! I was very upset.

We were all terribly sad. In the weeks that followed, I could not sleep. Two good, sweet young people had died, and it was all because of me and what I had done. I regretted everything that had happened, and I felt sick and **depressed**. I was also **terrified** because I knew that the monster might still be near us.

When August came, and two months had passed since Justine's death, I decided to go out walking for a few weeks in the mountains. I hoped that it would make me feel better. As I walked further, and climbed higher up the mountains, I felt lighter and freer. I saw Mont Blanc in front of me, and the blue skies and green valleys gave me some hope again.

One morning, I was alone and high up in the snowy mountains when it started to rain. The sky was dark, but I continued on my way and reached the top of Montanvert at around noon. I sat on a rock and looked down over a large, flat area of ice below me. After I had rested there for a while, I started to move across the area of ice. It was a little foggy now, so I moved slowly and carefully as I came down the side of the mountain.

Then, as the fog began to lift, I suddenly saw something on the other side of the snow and ice that was moving very quickly towards me. I saw that it was a man, and he was jumping easily over the rocks and big holes in the ice. I had a horrible shock when I realized that it was the creature! I felt very frightened, but I also felt very angry. This monster had killed my dear William, and Justine! I decided that I would fight him, and I waited for him to get near me.

"How can you come near me?" I shouted. "Aren't you scared that I will kill you, after what you have done?"

"I know that I am ugly and different, and most people hate me," he replied. "But you are the person who made me, and *you* talk about killing *me*? You, my creator, should give me what I need. If you do, then I will go away and live in peace. But if you **refuse**, then I will not disappear. I will continue to kill people."

"You monster! Yes, I created you, so I can kill you, too!" I cried, and I ran at him. But he easily jumped away from me.

"You made me bigger and stronger than you, but

I don't want to fight you," he told me. "Although you seem to hate me, I will not hate you. I was good and pure, but being alone and being hated has made me unhappy and dangerous. Give me what I need, and then I can be happy and safe again."

"Go away! Or fight me!" I shouted.

Now he spoke quietly. "Please be calm. You tell me I am bad because I've killed. But you now say you want to kill me. What's the difference? Please just listen to my story – that's all I ask. Come to the **cave** where I have been living these months, and hear me. Then, if you still want to kill me, do it. I shall not stop you."

As he said this, he started to walk across the ice, and I followed him. I did not answer him, but as we walked I thought about what he had said. I realized that he could be right – I was his creator, and perhaps I should think about his happiness before being quick to attack him. So I decided to do as he had asked. It was with great sadness that I followed him inside the cave and then sat down next to the fire that he had lit. It was then that he started to tell me his story.

CHAPTER SIX

The first months of life

In which the monster tells his story . . .

It is very difficult for me when I think about how my life began. Everything was new and frightening to me. All at once I could feel, see, smell and hear, and I did not know what to do. I started to move, and I discovered that I could walk. I went outside, but before I left your apartment I saw some clothes. I was cold and knew that I wanted to be covered, so I put them on. I walked and walked for hours, until I came to the forest at Ingolstadt. I felt very hungry and thirsty, so I found and ate some very small fruits and drank from the river.

After that, I fell down on the ground and went to sleep. Of course, it got dark, and when I awoke I felt frightened and lost. I sat on the ground and began to cry. Later I saw a round, white thing in the sky, and the beautiful light that came from it gave me hope.

I lived very simply in the forest, learning about myself and my body. I heard the wonderful song of birds, and I **survived** by eating leaves and plants. I saw how another great circle in the sky rose up each day and gave a very bright, yellow light, then slowly came down again and seemed to die.

Then, one evening, I found something hot and very bright on the ground. I think it had been left by some men.

I warmed myself by it and watched it for a long time. But when I reached out and touched it, I felt something horrible, and I pulled my hand back with a cry. I studied the hot thing carefully and saw that it was made of pieces of wood. I picked up as much wood as I could from the forest and put some on and near the fire. That was how I learned about fire and how it worked. But I was not experienced enough to keep it alive for longer than a day or two. I had also found an old coat near the fire. I used this to keep me dry when there was water coming down from the sky.

Many days passed, and I found it difficult to keep warm and find more food. It seemed to be getting colder, and I started to see lots of very cold, white areas on the ground. I started walking again, and several days later the snow had covered the ground everywhere I looked. Then, one morning, I found something square with a kind of door in it. I did not know it then, but it was a small **hut**. I gently pushed the door open and went in. An old man was sitting inside it, next to a fire, over which he was cooking his breakfast. When he turned and saw me, he screamed loudly, then jumped up and ran past me out of the hut.

I liked the hut – it was warm and dry, and there was no snow inside it. I was very hungry, so I ate all the food I could find there as quickly as I could. There was bread, cheese and milk, and I loved the taste and feel of these things in my mouth. With my stomach now full, I lay down

next to the fire and slept. When I woke up, I left the hut
and kept walking across the fields.

Some hours later, I arrived at a small village. I was excited
to see the vegetables growing in the gardens, and outside
some of the **cottage** windows I also saw milk and cheese.
I opened the door of one cottage and walked inside, but I
had only just put my foot inside when the children there
screamed in horror, and one of the women fainted and
fell to the floor. Soon everyone in the village was outside,
shouting and running after me, and some of them threw
stones at me. I ran away from them and out into the
country again.

Later that day, I found a very small wooden hut that was
next to a small cottage. There was nothing inside the hut,
and it had no door. I picked up some pieces of wood from
around the garden and used them to cover the place where
a door would be, and I used plants to make the inside of
it more comfortable. Although the little hut seemed to be
beginning to fall down, it was built against the cottage, and
the stones felt warm when I touched them. It was where the
fire was inside the cottage, so I could sit next to the wall and
keep myself warm.

I did not want to frighten the people in the cottage, so
I stayed inside the hut at first. There was a small hole that
I could look through, and I watched as a young woman
and a young man walked around outside the cottage. They
wore simple clothes and looked kind. Later, when it began
to get dark, I realized that there was a window in the wall

inside my hut but that it was covered with lots of pieces of wood. I carefully moved some of them, and then, through a small hole, I could see into the cottage. It was very simple inside, and I could see an old man. He seemed very sad and was sitting with his head in his hands. Later he picked something up and started to touch it. And it was then I heard something beautiful, which was similar to the sound I had heard the birds making in the forest.

I saw the three people looking at each other and smiling, and I felt something I had not felt before. There was a strange **mixture** of happiness and pain inside me. It was a strong feeling, and I had to look away from them.

I lived this way for a long time, watching the family and learning about their lives and how they talked to each other. I really wanted to share in their music, and to hear everything they said to each other, but I was too scared to show myself. Instead, I only came out of my hut in quiet moments, when I took pieces of food. Once I stole a small cup so that I could drink more easily from a little river nearby.

The young man and woman worked very hard, but they did not have much food to eat. I came to understand that they were very poor, and that they had a more difficult life than the people in the village. I also slowly realized that the old man was blind and could see nothing at all.

CHAPTER SEVEN

Learning new things

I liked these people very much, and so I decided to try to help them. I stopped stealing food from the cottage, and instead I found plants and fruits from the forest. I saw that the young man always spent a lot of his time working hard to find and cut wood for the fire. So, during the night, I used to go into the forest and collect as much wood as I could for him. I remember, the first time I did this, the young woman opened the front door of the cottage the next morning. When she saw the pieces of wood she looked surprised and very happy, and she ran inside and told the other two people, who laughed and cried with happiness. I very much liked seeing and hearing this. I also saw that the young man did not go into the forest that day to work but stayed near his family and spent a little time relaxing.

I was hungry to know more about these people and their world. During the day I carefully watched and listened to the three of them as they moved about the cottage and garden. I started to understand some of the words that they used a lot, for example, "fire", "milk", "bread" and "wood".

After a few more days I knew their names – the young woman was "Agatha" or "sister", and the young man's name was "Felix" or "brother", and also sometimes "son". The old man was always called "father". I wanted to learn

all these words, and so I quietly repeated them again and again to myself in my hut.

In the evenings they often sat near the fire and talked or played music. Felix sometimes took out something small and square, which seemed to be a very special thing. I noticed how he gently touched it and looked after it very carefully. He used to open it and then talk on his own for a long time, while the other two listened. I later realized that Felix was reading aloud from a book, and that the words were written on the page in front of him. So this was how I spent the whole winter: watching, listening and learning everything I could from this little family that I had grown to love.

Then, one day, I found a small lake in the woods, and I saw myself in the calm, flat water. I was shocked and jumped back – I was ugly and frightening, and I did not look like any of the people I had seen. My heart was heavy, and I returned to my hut worried and upset. Later that night I decided that I would study harder and learn to speak their language. In this way, I hoped to one day be like them and speak like them, so that they would not be frightened of me.

Soon the weather started to change and become warmer, and the evenings became lighter. There were different plants and flowers in the forest, and I saw Felix collecting more vegetables from the garden. During this time I learned a lot, and every night I repeated again and again all the words and **phrases** I had noted that day.

Sometimes Felix read from stories, and other times he read from different types of books. I started to understand a lot more, and I learned about history, geography, money, big houses and cities, kings, friends, families and the birth and growth of children, and many other things. I already knew that I looked very different to everyone else. Now, of course, I realized that I had no money, and I had no house. And there were lots of difficult questions in my head. Had I ever been a young child? Where were my friends and family? If I was not like these people, what was I? I felt sadder than ever before.

Soon after this, I was exploring deep in the forest one night when I found a bag. Inside it were three big books and some clothes. Excited and happy, I brought the bag back to my hut. I spent the next days and weeks studying the books and teaching myself to read. It was hard work, and I did not understand a lot of it, but I really wanted to learn everything I could.

It was at that time that I remembered something important. All those months ago, when I first arrived at the little cottage, I had discovered some papers in the pocket of the clothes that I had taken from your laboratory. But now I remembered those papers, and I looked at them again and studied them very carefully. I was shocked by what I read. In them you described all the things you had done to make me – the whole story of my awful creation was there on the pages for me to read. You wrote that I was horrible and ugly, and you said that I was your biggest mistake. I felt sick when I read it all.

After this, I became very depressed. My only hope, I believed, was to try to talk to Felix, Agatha and their father. If I could tell them my story, perhaps they would understand me and be my friends? I decided that I would spend the next few months getting ready to meet them. I would practise my reading and my speaking, and I would learn everything I could to give myself the best chance.

Autumn came and then passed, and I learned more and more each day. Some days I was excited and hopeful when I thought about my plan to meet the small family. Other days I felt **miserable** and believed that they would hate me and make me leave the cottage. Yet every day my feelings for them grew. I loved watching them as they looked after each other and shared things together. I wanted to feel what they felt.

When the winter came again, I decided that I was ready. I had made a plan – I would wait until Felix and Agatha were away from the cottage, and then I would speak to the old man alone. I hoped that, because he was blind, he would be able to listen to me. I wanted him to get to know me without being frightened or shocked by how I looked.

CHAPTER EIGHT
From good to bad

One cold day soon after, Agatha and Felix went on a long walk together, leaving their father alone in the cottage. I saw my chance. I felt very nervous, but I walked to the front door of the cottage and knocked.

"Who's there?" said the man. "Come in!"

I went in. "Please excuse me," I said. "I'm a traveller who needs some rest. Could I come in from the cold and warm myself by the fire?" He nodded, and then he told me that he was blind. He said that he was sorry but, because he could not see, he was not able to get me anything to eat. "That's fine. I'm not hungry," I replied. "I would just like to rest, keep warm and talk a little."

I sat down by the fire and explained that I was alone and poor, and that I did not have any friends or family. "That is very sad," he said. "But please don't worry. I'm sure you will find friends. Isn't there anyone you know who could be a friend to you?"

"There is a family that I care very much about," I told him. "They are wonderful people, but I don't think they want to be my friends. I'm a very good person – I am kind and helpful – but I'm very ugly, and I've lived a very different life. Because of that, they probably won't want to know me."

The old man thought for a moment and then spoke.

45

"But, surely, if you really are a good man, then when they talk to you and understand that, their view will change."

I told him that I was about to talk to them. I explained that I had helped them and got to know them over the last few months, and that I really hoped that they would not be scared of me.

"Where do these people live?" he asked. I told him that they lived nearby.

"You seem to be a good, honest man. Perhaps I can help you. I might be able to tell them that I know you. Tell me a little about them. What are their names?"

I did not know what to say. This was the important chance I had been waiting for, but I was terrified. It was all too much for me, and I said nothing but started to cry loudly. It was then that I heard Agatha and Felix talking as they returned to the cottage.

I quickly held the old man's hand and told him, "Now is the time! Please save me! Please help me! It is you – you and your family – that I was telling you about. You are the people I really want to be friends with!"

"What?" the man cried. "Who are you?"

At that moment the door opened, and Agatha and Felix walked in. Oh, it was **horrific**! I regretted ever thinking it might be possible to be friends with them. When Agatha saw me she screamed and fainted, while Felix immediately ran over to where I was sitting.

He pulled me away from his father and on to the floor before hitting me as hard as he could with a large stick. I was strong enough to kill him, but I chose not fight him. When he lifted the stick again, planning to hit me again, I quickly stood up and ran out of the cottage. Luckily I managed to return to my hut and hide without being noticed.

Oh! How awful and miserable that day was! I was full of **rage** and hate. That night, after dark, I ran far into the forest, shouting and screaming, and hitting anything that got in my way. I decided that I hated all people, but, most of all, I hated you. You were the one who had created me and had not looked after me. I read your papers again and discovered from them that you lived in Geneva. I wanted **revenge**. I wanted to find you and kill you, so I planned to return to Geneva as soon as I could.

I began my journey as winter came, and there was snow on the ground. I was careful to travel mostly at night so that people would not see me. The journey was long and hard, but I had no choice – I was angry and needed to find you. And the closer I got to you, the more deeply I felt my pain and rage.

At last, on a summer's evening, I arrived in Geneva and knew that I was near you.

I was resting in a small forest by the road when a young boy came running into the area where I was sitting. I suddenly thought that, because he was so young, perhaps he had not yet learned to hate anyone who looked different to him. Could I possibly teach him to like and help me? I quickly reached out and caught him. But, as soon as he saw me, he screamed loudly.

"You horrible monster!" he cried. "Let me go, or I'll tell my father!"

"You won't see your father again," I told him as I carried him away.

"Let me go! My father is Mr Frankenstein, and he'll come and find you!" he shouted.

"Frankenstein?" I was shocked and full of anger. "Then you belong to my enemy, and I'm going to kill you!"

The boy fought me and shouted horrific things about me. I wanted him to stop shouting, so I put my hands around his neck. Soon the shouting stopped, and he lay dead on the ground at my feet. I looked down at the body and felt a strange happiness, because I knew that the boy's death would be a terrible thing for you, my creator. Then, as I was looking at the boy, I saw something around his neck. It was a very small picture of a very beautiful woman.

I took it off his neck. Looking at it made me feel warm inside – maybe it was the woman's calm and beautiful eyes – so I put the picture in my pocket. But then I remembered everything that had happened to me, and how I would never be able to have anyone to love, or to love me! I felt very upset and ran away, leaving the boy's body on the ground.

Soon I found an old farm building, and I went inside to rest. But, when I entered, I saw that there was a young woman sleeping on the ground. Like all the other people I had met, she would surely scream and run away if she woke up and saw me. Why could no one see the real me?

I felt angry, and I wanted to punish her for it. So I took the little picture, and I put it in her pocket instead of mine. Now, if anyone found it, she would be seen as the murderer of the boy!

I stayed nearby for several days, hoping to see you, before I came to the mountains. I want you to do something for me. I am depressed and lonely. I need a **female** to share my life with, and she must be like me. You must help me with this!

CHAPTER NINE
The promise

In which Victor Frankenstein continues his story . . .

The creature finished speaking and looked at me. He was waiting for me to reply, but I was shocked and confused. I was not really sure what he was asking me to do. Then he spoke again.

"You must create a woman, a woman who is like me. If she is like me, then she will not think I am ugly, and she will truly love and understand me. You created me, and so you must do this for me. It is my **right** to ask for this."

When he had told me about his life with the family at the cottage, I had felt very sad. But the last part of his story had made me very angry again. "No!" I said. "I will not do it. And I don't care what you do to me. I will never make another dangerous, murdering creature like you!"

"Yet I am the one who is talking calmly and wants to make peace," he replied. "And you are the one who wants to kill me. If you killed me, then you would be a murderer, and you would be the same as me. Except that you have a loving family and friends, and can live happily in the world. I cannot be happy, not without another creature who is like me. I am miserable. Give me a woman like me, who will understand and love me, and all my anger will disappear. I will live in peace, and you will never see me or hear of me again. But, if you refuse, then I have no hope. And if I cannot give love, then instead I will give hate. And, most of all, I will hate you. So, I ask again: will you do it?"

I felt sad listening to him. In many ways he was right, and the words he used showed that he was intelligent and that he had deep feelings. But, when I looked at him, I also saw what a horrible and shocking monster he was. There was a mixture of feelings inside me, and I did not know what to say. I thought very carefully before I replied.

"If I do what you ask, will you promise me one thing?" I asked him. "Will you leave Europe and go somewhere far, far away from all people with your new friend?"

"Yes! I promise by the sun, by the moon, and by the fire of love that burns in my heart!" he cried. "Please go home and start your work. I will watch, and, when I see that you have finished, I shall appear." Then he stood up and left.

I watched from the mouth of the cave as he ran down the side of the mountain and then was gone. It had taken several hours for him to tell me his story, and now it was beginning to get dark. As I walked down the mountain, I thought about what he had said and everything that now needed to happen. I was very upset and started to cry. Oh! What a terrible thing I had agreed to do!

I returned home to Geneva as quickly as I could. Of course, I could not tell my family what had happened, but they could see how ill and worried I looked. I knew that, to keep my family safe, I needed to do what I had promised. I also knew that it would be much harder to make a **female** creature. But many weeks passed by, and I could not make myself start the horrible job. How could I do that terrible thing in my family home? Then, one day, I heard that there were some scientists in England who had made some important discoveries. Perhaps that new information would help me. So I told my father that I needed to go to England to study exciting new science there. It was decided that I would go to England for a year, and, when I returned, Elizabeth and I would be married. Oh! I could not wait for the day when I would be free of the monster and be able to marry Elizabeth and start a new life.

It was at the end of September that, with a heavy heart, I left Elizabeth behind and began my journey to England. My good friend Henry Clerval travelled with me, and I was pleased about this. The creature had said that he was going to watch and follow me, and perhaps I would be safer if Clerval came with me. We travelled in carriages, and on boats and ships, and we looked out on the very beautiful places that we passed. Clerval seemed to be the happiest man alive, because he often talked excitedly about his plans for England, while I usually stayed silent. I was too miserable to laugh and talk with my friend. It was the end of October when we finally arrived in England. It was my first time visiting the country, and we decided to stay in London for several months.

While we were in London, I contacted the scientists I

needed to see, and I discovered lots of useful information from them. Of course, I told Clerval nothing of my true plans, and I never said anything about the creature to him. Clerval had his own interests, and sometimes many days passed without us seeing each other.

In March, we decided to travel to Scotland. Clerval wanted to see its wild beauty, and I liked the fact that it was far away and few people lived there. It would be the perfect place for me to make the female creature in secret. We stopped and visited many places on the way, including Windsor, Oxford and the famous lakes in the north of England. We finally arrived in Scotland in July.

We knew some people in Perth, and they had invited us to visit. I saw my chance to be alone and start my awful work. Clerval planned to stay with these people, but I told him I would now travel around Scotland on my own for a few months. I was beginning to get worried. Had the monster been following me? Would he be angry that I had not yet started making his female friend?

I travelled to the furthest part of Scotland and took a boat to a small island. It felt like the right place to do my work – it was five miles out to sea, and it was rocky, so not many plants and trees grew there. Only five people lived on the island, but I managed to rent an old, falling-down cottage where I could live.

And so it was that I made myself another laboratory and finally started my work. Every morning I worked on the female creature, and every evening I walked along the

shore of the rocky beach and looked at the wild ocean. I hated my work, and I hated being alone in this miserable place, but I had no choice. I thought only about finishing this second, new creature, and about the day when I would have to see the first one again.

CHAPTER TEN

The creature returns

It was about nine months later that I was sitting in my laboratory one evening, looking up at the full moon high in the sky. I was thinking about the monster. It had been about three years earlier that I had started to make the first creature in my laboratory in Ingolstadt. I had not known what he would be like, and I did not know what this female creature would be like either. My head was now full of questions. What would I do if the female creature was more dangerous than the first monster? He had promised to go far away, and keep away from people. But his new female friend had not. If she wanted to kill people, it would be very difficult to stop her. What would the monster do if the new female hated him? What would happen if they had children together and created more dangerous monsters? I suddenly saw the seriousness of what I was doing, and I felt sick. Could I refuse to do it? If I decided wrongly, perhaps many more bad things would happen.

At that moment, I looked up and saw, through the window, the monster standing outside in the light of the moon. He seemed to have a horrible smile on his face as he looked in and saw me sitting behind the table in my laboratory.

On the table he could see the female creature that

I was working on. Yes, this monster really had followed me across Europe. He had hidden in forests and caves and had watched me carefully. And here he was, and he knew that his female friend was almost ready for him. But, oh! What had I done? I suddenly felt that I had made a terrible mistake, and I was filled with regret. I stood up, and, shaking with rage, I immediately started to damage the female creature. I pulled pieces from her, I hit her and I threw her to the floor. When he saw what I was doing, the monster screamed and then ran away.

I left the room and locked it, and then I made a promise to myself. I would never make another creature again. Then I went to my bedroom, but I could not sleep. Several hours later, I heard the front door of my cottage moving. I was terrified, but there was nothing I could do. Moments later, the bedroom door opened, and the monster walked slowly into my room. He whispered in a slow, angry voice.

"I have followed you across Europe. I have waited patiently for months. But now you have damaged what you created. What are you trying to do? Have you broken your promise to me?"

"Yes," I replied. "I have broken my promise. I will never again make another creature. I cannot! Now go away!"

He was full of anger and hate as he looked at me. "So every man can have a wife, but not me? Must I be alone for ever? That's not fair! You will pay for this. I will make you sorry!"

"I will not change my mind," I told him. "Go! Leave me alone!"

"I will go," he said, quietly. "But remember this – I will be with you on your wedding night."

"You monster!" I shouted at him. "Before you say you are going to kill me, be sure you are safe yourself first!"

I jumped towards him, but he turned and ran out of the cottage. I hurried outside and saw him push a small boat out into the ocean and climb into it.

I remembered his last words to me. Would he kill me on my wedding day? Poor, sweet Elizabeth! I could not let her see me die in front of her. So I thought of a plan.

The next morning, when the sun began to rise in the sky, I made myself go into the laboratory to collect the body parts together and put them in a large basket. I carefully cleaned all the scientific objects that I had used for my experiments, and I packed them into cases. Then, in the evening, with some difficulty, I took the basket outside to the beach, where I put some heavy stones inside it, too.

I waited until very late at night, and then I put the heavy basket into a little sailing boat. I sailed it about four miles out to sea, and as I did so I became more and more nervous. Then I lowered the sail and pushed the large basket and what was inside it into the ocean. It quickly disappeared down into the dark water. I felt pleased when I had done it, and I lay back on the floor of the boat.

I was very tired, and in just a few minutes I fell deeply asleep.

I do not know how long I lay sleeping there, but when I woke up the sun was high in the sky. I was out on the Atlantic Ocean, and I could not see land anywhere. I looked around me and saw that it was windy now, and the water was no longer calm. Many hours passed, and I felt very sick as the boat moved up and down and from side to side. Would I survive? Or would I die from hunger and thirst alone in that small boat? Then, just as it was beginning to get dark, I saw land. I was so happy! The land looked rocky, and different to where I had come from. But, as I sailed nearer, I saw that there was a small town. When I began to pull the boat out of the water and up on to the shore, some men appeared and started walking towards me. I thought they were going to help me, but instead they stopped and stood in a group and whispered to one another.

I called to them. "My good friends! Please can you tell me where I am?"

"You'll know soon enough," one of the men replied.

"Why do you answer so rudely? I thought the English are well known for being polite and welcoming strangers."

"Well, you aren't in England now," the man said. "You are in Ireland. And we Irish don't like murderers."

"Murderers?" I repeated, shocked by what he had said.

"Yes. Come with me. We want to hear your story about the death of a man who was found murdered here last night."

I could not believe what was happening. I did not know

anything about this dead man! I had been alone on the boat since last night. But I had no choice – I had to go with this crowd and answer their questions.

I have to stop for a moment now because I must feel strong to remember and describe the truly awful things that happened next.

CHAPTER ELEVEN
A terrible shock

I was taken to a large, important-looking building in the centre of the town. It was there that I was introduced to the **magistrate**, an old man who was sitting at the front of the main room. Another man stepped forward and started to describe what he had seen the night before. He told the story of how he had gone fishing with two other men, and how they had discovered a dead body on the beach when they returned later that evening.

"Describe exactly what you saw," the magistrate said.

"The body was of a handsome young man of about twenty-five years of age," replied the fisherman. "His clothes were dry, and he had no cuts on him or damage to his clothes. But there were black marks of fingers all around his neck."

When I heard these words, I remembered the murder of my brother, and I felt sick. I was very shocked, and I had to sit down. The magistrate noticed this and stared at me for a moment or two, before turning back to the fisherman.

"Did you see anyone nearby that evening?"

"Yes. Just before we found the body, we saw a small boat in the water, not far from the shore. The boat was being sailed away from the beach by one man. There wasn't much light – just a little from the moon – but I think it was the same boat that I saw this man arrive in." And, as he said this, he pointed straight at me. There was silence in the room as the magistrate thought about what he had heard.

"Let's show him the body," he said at last. "I want to watch him when he sees it. Follow me." Of course, I had seen many dead bodies in my scientific work, so I was not frightened of this. I was more worried about the fact that I needed to somehow show them that I really was **innocent**.

Two of the fishermen took me by the arms, and we were immediately led to the room where the body lay. How can I describe the feelings I had when I saw that dead body? Even now, I feel sick and miserable just thinking about it. Everything that had happened that day, and all the worrying thoughts I had in my mind, were gone in a moment. I saw that it was the body of my dear friend Henry Clerval lying on the table in front of me.

I threw myself on him and cried out, "Oh! Two other people have already been killed! And now you are dead, my dearest, good friend. And it's all because of my murderous work!" The pain was too great for me, and I fainted. I was then carried from the room, and I don't remember what happened next. I became extremely ill and lay for two months in bed. I could not eat, and I had horrible nightmares about the monster, William, Justine and Henry. Then one day I woke up feeling a little calmer. I looked around the small, white room I was in and saw that it was empty except for the bed, and I then found that the door was locked. I was in prison! Slowly some of the memories of what had happened came back to me.

Several days later, the magistrate came to visit me. He was a kind man and seemed to want to help me. I listened carefully as he spoke. "I'm sorry that you are being kept in this awful prison. I have read all the papers that you had with you when you were found, and I don't believe that you are guilty. I think that you were in the wrong place at the wrong time, and I hope that new information will soon be found that shows you are innocent."

I listened carefully as he spoke. "In your papers, I also found a letter from your father, which had his address on it. So when you were first imprisoned I wrote to him, but I never received a reply." With this, the magistrate stood up and walked to the door. He opened it and said, "But now there is someone who has come to see you."

"My father!" I cried. I had never been so pleased to see someone in my whole life. We spent a short time together, and he told me that he and Elizabeth were both well. In the days that followed I became a little stronger, but I was still miserable and ill.

A month later, I was called to go to **court**, which was in a town almost 100 miles away. All the information was read aloud, and lots of different reports were shown to the court. One report said that people had seen me on the Scottish island at the time when Clerval's body was found, many miles away in Ireland. Oh! How happy my father was when the court decided that I was innocent! Yet I myself was not very happy to hear the news. My life would be miserable anyway, whether I was in prison or not. How could I ever be happy again? Many of the people I loved dearly had died horrific deaths: William, Justine and Henry. The monster now wanted to kill me, and my father and Elizabeth were not safe either.

I was still very weak and thin, but my father and I decided to begin the long, slow journey back to Geneva. I wanted to return there as fast as possible in order to look after the lives of those whom I loved. I knew that the monster was likely to appear there again, too. If he ever did return, then I would definitely kill him. I was now completely sure. I would never again feel sorry for him after what he had done, and I could think of nothing else. Every time I slept I had awful nightmares about his creation, and I saw his face, with its horrible smile, and his arm reaching out to me. There were days when I spent much of my time crying. But, of course, I could not share my true pain and my story with my father.

He would surely hate me and would never forgive me if he knew that I had created a horrible monster that had killed his youngest son, murdered Clerval, and also caused the death of Justine.

Weeks later, we arrived in Paris, and a letter came from Elizabeth.

18th May 1796, Geneva

Dear Victor,

I am very pleased that you have reached Paris. You are not far from me! I really hope that you are feeling much better now. There is something I need to ask you before you return. We both know that our family has wanted us to marry each other since we were children. But for many, many months now you have been far from me studying in Ingolstadt, and now you are studying and travelling in England and Scotland. I need to know how you feel about me. Is there another woman that you love? I love you and want to marry you, but most of all I want you to be happy. If you can only be happy with another, then that is what needs to happen.

With all my love,
Elizabeth Lavenza

I thought about my dear, sweet Elizabeth, and I felt a little happier. She was my hope for the future. If I could kill the monster, perhaps Elizabeth's love could save me. I wrote a reply to her immediately.

26th May 1796, Geneva

My dear Elizabeth,

I love you and want to marry you, and you do not need to worry. But I must tell you that I have a very big secret, which has been too terrible for me to share with you. When you know what it is, you will understand why I have been away from you, and why I have been so miserable. I promise that I shall tell you everything on the day after we are married.

With much love,
Victor Frankenstein

We arrived in Geneva a week later, and I was very happy to see Elizabeth's smiling face. We decided to get married as soon as possible. My feelings were a mixture of excitement about marrying Elizabeth, and being terribly frightened that the monster would then come and kill me. Soon the day came, and she and I were married. How wonderful that she was now my wife! We happily said goodbye to my father and then left that same afternoon to go on holiday and stay in an inn up in the mountains. But, secretly, I carried a gun with me and watched carefully as we began our journey.

The wedding night

As Elizabeth and I travelled along in the carriage, with the sun on our faces, I felt happier than I had in many months. But this happiness did not last. It was 8 p.m., and the sun was beginning to go down when we arrived at the lake in the Alps. I started to feel very nervous, and I remembered again the monster's last words to me: "I will be with you on your wedding night."

We went for a short walk along the shore of the lake before dinner, but I was very nervous, and I kept my hand on the gun, which I carried secretly inside my jacket. Every small sound worried me, and I could not relax. A strong wind began to rise as we walked, and then the sun disappeared completely and we could then see the full moon high up in the sky. Clouds moved quickly across it, sometimes covering the moon and making it darker, and sometimes letting the moonlight shine brightly on the lake.

Elizabeth seemed uncomfortable, and she kept looking at me. "Why are you so nervous, Victor?" she asked, finally. "What are you afraid of?"

"Please don't worry, my love," I told her, trying to sound calm. "Tonight is a terrible night – just this one night. Then, I promise you, I will be able to relax, and everything will be fine. I promise that I will explain everything tomorrow."

It was then that suddenly I realized that a fight with the

monster would be an awful, frightening thing for Elizabeth to see. I did not want her to see that, whatever happened.

"It's been a long day. We are both tired. Why don't you go to our room and get some rest? I will come soon," I told her. When she had gone, I spent some time walking all around the outside of the inn, looking for any sign of the monster, but I found nothing. Then I checked all around the inside the building itself and made sure that the front door was locked behind me. I was just deciding if I needed to do anything more when I heard a loud and awful scream from our room, where Elizabeth was resting. As I heard that scream, the whole truth rushed into my mind, and my mouth fell open in shock. For a moment I could not move as I tried to understand it all. Then there came a second scream, which immediately woke me from my shock. I rushed as fast as I could into the bedroom.

Oh! It was so horrific! Why did I not die in that terrible moment?

Why am I still alive now to describe the horrible death of the most beautiful, most loving woman on earth? The room was silent now, and she was lying there, thrown across the bed, with her head hanging down towards the floor.

Her beautiful face looked very different. It was white, and half-covered with her long hair. I will never forget seeing her lying there on the bed like that, dead. The awful picture fills my mind even now. I was almost unable to breathe, and I stood staring at her for a moment before I rushed over and took her in my arms. I was shocked that

her skin already felt a little cold, and, suddenly, the body no longer seemed to be Elizabeth, whom I had known so well and had loved very dearly.

It was then that I saw something move, and I turned to look at the window. I had not noticed before, but the curtains were pulled back, and the window was open. And there, standing outside the window in the moonlight, was the monster. I saw a horrible smile appear on his face, and then he lifted his hand and pointed at the body of my wife.

I was immediately filled with anger and hate. I stood up and took the gun from my jacket. As quickly as I could, I pointed it towards him and fired a shot. But he was too fast for me, and he turned and ran away from the inn towards the lake, and I saw him run into the water. The other people staying at the inn heard the gunshot and came running into the room.

I described the monster, and I pointed to where he had run. I am sure that these men thought I was mad and did not believe what I had described. We **chased** after him and searched for hours, and some of the men went out in boats to look for him, but we found nothing.

During all of this I felt sick, and it seemed like I was living in a terrible nightmare. All I could think of was that William had been killed, Justine had been hanged, Clerval murdered and now my wife taken from me in this horrible, shocking way. When would all this end? And what about my father? Was he safe? Or would he be the next to die?

I decided to return to Geneva as quickly as I could.

I will not tell you all the things that happened on the way, nor what I was thinking and feeling. You have heard enough of my story to know how horrific it all was. I arrived home and saw that my father was safe, but he was extremely sad and upset when I told him what had happened to his dear Elizabeth. This last death was too much for him, and he stopped eating and became very depressed and ill. He was already very old and a little weak, and a few days later he **gave up** and died in my arms. The last person in my family was gone! Oh, how I hated the monster!

What then happened to me? I do not know. I lost the ability to feel, and darkness and **depression** closed in around me.

Many months later, when I was calmer and the shock of it all had passed, I realized that I was in a special room. They had called me mad and kept me there for my own safety. I began to think carefully about everything that had happened, and, the more I thought about it, the angrier I got. I wanted to make sure other people were safe, but, more than anything, I wanted my revenge against that hateful creature!

CHAPTER THIRTEEN
The chase

When I felt better and was allowed to go back out into the world, I decided that I needed someone who could help me. I went to see a well-known magistrate in Geneva and began to tell him my story. First I gave him the most important pieces of information – I described the four deaths and how they had happened. I also told him that I knew the person who was the killer.

"Don't worry," he told me. "I promise you that I will do everything in my power to find this awful murderer."

But, when I gave him more information and told him who the creature was and all the things that had happened over the last few years, he looked at me in shock. He did not seem to believe it.

"I'm sorry, but this is all very strange, and I cannot really help you," he said. "Nobody could chase and catch a strange animal that can run and jump over rivers and kill people in the way that you have described. And many months have passed since these murders. This wild creature could be anywhere in the world by now."

"If you refuse to help me, then you give me no choice," I told him. "I must follow this monster myself. I will find and kill him alone. I will not give up!"

I left the magistrate full of rage and with a real need for revenge. To be honest, I think I was still quite ill at that time. But I had decided, and I soon left Geneva and started my search for the monster.

And now I am here with you in the Arctic Ocean, far, far away from home. And my searching will go on until I find the monster and kill him, or until I die, whichever of those things comes sooner. I have travelled across a large part of the world and have experienced all kinds of problems on the way. I do not know how I have survived the cold, the danger and the horrible places I have been to. Many times I have lain down on the ground and wanted to die, but revenge has made me carry on. I just cannot die and leave my enemy alive.

At first, I knew that the monster must be in or near Geneva, but I did not know where. On the night I left home and started my search, I went to the place where William, Elizabeth and my father were **buried**. Although they were dead, I wanted to talk to them and say goodbye to them, as I knew it may be many months before I returned to Geneva, if I ever did.

I felt very upset as I stood and spoke aloud to them. "My dear family. Here and now I promise you that I will chase this terrible monster, and I will keep chasing him until I have killed him, or he has killed me. I *will* get revenge for our family!" At that moment I was answered by a loud and horrible laugh. Somebody was hiding in the darkness! When the laugh ended, I heard that hateful voice that I knew well, and it spoke to me in a loud whisper from somewhere nearby.

"I am happy that you have decided to live, you miserable, selfish man."

The moon had come out from behind a cloud now, and I quickly looked all around for the monster. I could not find him anywhere, but then I suddenly saw him in the moonlight running as fast as the wind away from me. I chased him, and for many months I followed him. It became my job, and it was all that I could think about. Often I lost him, but then I would find him again by asking people if they had seen a strange creature. Other times he would leave a sign or a message because he did not want me to lose him. I followed him along the river Rhone, and then I saw him getting on a ship that was going to the Black Sea. Then I chased him through the wild parts of Russia, where there was snow on the ground, and I could see his huge steps and follow the path he had taken more easily.

These last few months have been extremely difficult. I have eaten and drunk where I could, but I have often been extremely hungry and thirsty. I have felt alone, lost and depressed, but I have kept going because of the anger and revenge I feel. I do not know what the monster is thinking or feeling. He can survive when it is extremely cold. He knows I cannot do that. I think he has brought me here for that reason and wants to make me **suffer** as much as he can. But here on the huge areas of ice there is nowhere to hide, and, when I bought a sledge and dogs, I hoped that I could finally catch and kill him. I do not know how many days have passed since then, but, by the amount of food

I brought with me and had finished several days before you found me, I think it was about three weeks. I had got closer to him, and I had seen him on his sledge not more than a mile in front of me. But then the weather turned bad.

The ice began moving under me, and, suddenly, with a terribly loud noise, it broke in front of me, and a big open area of water started to open up. I was shocked to see that I was now on a piece of ice, with open ocean all around me.

Many awful hours passed, and all of my dogs died. I gave up all hope, but then I saw your ship about a mile away from me. I quickly broke some large pieces of wood from the sledge and used them in the water to move the piece of ice slowly towards you. I decided that, if you were travelling south, I would ask you for a small boat in which to continue my journey. Luckily for me you are going north, so I am able to carry on travelling north and looking for the monster. But, Walton, please promise me something. I am weak and very thin, and I am not well. If I die, and you see this monster on your travels, will you kill him for me? He speaks very intelligently, but you must not trust him. Do not listen to him, but instead remember the names of William, Justine, Clerval, Elizabeth, my father and myself – Victor – and then kill him. Push your knife into his heart!

CHAPTER FOURTEEN
The ship returns

In which Robert Walton writes another letter . . .

26th August

So, dear Margaret, you have now read this strange and amazing story.
It is very frightening, isn't it? Sometimes Victor Frankenstein was so
upset and in so much pain that he could not continue his story and began
to cry instead. Other times he was filled with anger and almost shouted
his words.

Although it seems impossible, I believe his story. He showed me some
documents, and I saw for myself the huge, strange-looking creature on the
other sledge. I'm very interested in this creature. Can it be possible that
Frankenstein has really created this amazing living thing? I think it is.
I have asked him to explain to me how he did it, but he refuses to tell me.

"Are you mad, my friend?" he said. "Why do you want to know?
Do you want to create for yourself and the world another dangerous
monster? No. Learn by my terrible mistakes, and do not ask to know
more about this."

Frankenstein saw that I was writing notes as he spoke – he asked
to see them and has read and corrected them, and he has also added
information in some places. It has taken a whole week for him to tell me
the whole story, and I have listened carefully to every word.

He has become a friend to me, and I want to help him, and yet he is *so miserable and so upset by all the awful things that have happened to him. We do not always talk about his horrific experiences. He is very intelligent and knows a lot about many different subjects. But he has given up on life and is so damaged, and has known so much pain, that I am frightened he cannot be saved.*

2nd September

My dear sister,

I write to you not knowing whether I will ever again see England. There is a lot of ice around the ship, and now we can hardly move. The sailors come to me wanting me to give them news, but I have none to give. It is my job to lead and look after these men, and to keep them safe. And, if something bad does happen here, then what about you? You would wait for years and years and hear nothing, and you would never know what happened to us. I do hope this ice moves soon and we are able to continue our journey.

5th September

*We are still in the middle of huge mountains of ice. Several of my men
have already died from the cold, and Frankenstein has become thinner
and seems more unwell every day. Many of the sailors are now calling
for us to turn around and return to Russia if we manage to move away
from this ice. But I am not sure. I think I would rather die out here than
give up and return home not having made any new discoveries.*

12th September

*I have decided. We are returning to England. I have lost all hope of
success and fame, and I have lost my friend. I will describe what
has happened here, my dear sister, while I am slowly sailing towards
England and towards you.*

*On 9th September, the ice began to move with sounds as loud as
thunder. It was dangerous, but we were lucky and the ship was not
damaged. The ice broke, and then the ship was able to move freely.
The sailors now all wanted to go home, and I could not refuse them
any longer. Frankenstein was now very weak, and when he heard this
news he was upset and became more unwell. I sat next to his bed, and
again he asked me, "Will you find and kill the monster? I cannot now
do it myself. I am ready to die. And if you will not do this, then look for
happiness in life and do not try to be great and famous."*

*He held my hand, and his voice became quieter as he spoke, and then,
thirty minutes or so later, his eyes closed for ever.*

Margaret, what can I say that will tell you how sad I now feel? I am crying, and I feel miserable, but at least I am returning to you.

Oh, wait. There are some noises, and I need to go and check . . . I can hear a voice coming from where Frankenstein's body lies. I will write more soon. Goodnight, my dear sister.

———————

Oh! I can hardly describe what has just happened! But I must, because it is the end of this horrific story.

I entered the room where my friend's body lay. Something . . . someone . . . enormous and very strange was standing over him. One arm was reaching out towards Frankenstein, and I could see the skin on the huge arm, and it was yellow and horrible. He was quietly talking to Frankenstein's body, but, when he heard me behind him, he stopped talking. He turned, and I saw the full horror of his ugly face.

"This is the end of it all," he cried. "Oh, Frankenstein, my creator, I came to ask you to forgive me for bringing you to your death by killing all those people whom you loved. But now you are cold and cannot answer me!"

At first I had planned to kill the creature as my friend had asked me. But now I was filled with interest. I was frightened, but I managed to speak. "It is too late for regrets now. Why did you not feel something for him all those months ago?"

"Oh, but I did!" he replied. "I spoke to him in peace, and I asked him to help me, but he would not. All I wanted was to have a family, or a friend, but now he is dead.

"I have spent my life alone and sad. Every person who sees me hates

me and is scared of me. How can I possibly have lived without anger, pain and revenge? And now it has all come to an end. But there is one more thing that I must do. I will leave this ship and go to the north, where I will collect wood and make a huge fire. On it I will burn myself and die. I will find peace and happiness in death, and I, and Frankenstein, will both be forgotten. Goodbye!"

He jumped from the window of the ship as he said this, and landed on a large piece of ice below. He was soon carried away by the sea, and he was lost in darkness.

During-reading questions

Write the answers to these questions in your notebook.

CHAPTER ONE

1 Why is Robert Walton travelling to the North Pole?
2 What two strange things do the sailors see from the ship?
3 Why is the new gentleman on the ship sad?

CHAPTER TWO

1 What happens to the big tree near Victor Frankenstein's house?
2 What new information does young Victor learn after that, and what effect does it have on him?
3 Who dies in this chapter, and why?

CHAPTER THREE

1 How do you think Victor feels during his first two years at university?
2 Why does Victor study dead human bodies?
3 What does Victor decide that he wants to achieve once he has discovered the secret of life?

CHAPTER FOUR

1 Why does Victor say that he has been "stupid"?
2 What does Victor see in his bedroom, and what does he do as a result?
3 Who helps Victor? How does that person help him?

CHAPTER FIVE

1 What is the "bad news" that begins this chapter?
2 Why is Victor full of regret after the death of Justine?
3 How do Victor's feelings towards the creature change during this chapter?

CHAPTER SIX

1 In the first few days of his life ...
   a what does the creature eat?
   b what does he drink?
   c how does he keep warm?
2 What important things do you think the creature learns by watching the family who live in the cottage?

CHAPTER SEVEN

1 How does the creature help the family in the cottage?
2 Who had written the papers that the creature has in his pocket?
3 How does the creature feel when he reads the papers? Why does he feel these things?

CHAPTER EIGHT

1 How does the creature feel at the beginning of this chapter? And how does he feel at the end of it?
2 Who is the boy in the forest, whom the creature kills?
3 Who is the young woman who is sleeping in an old farm building?

CHAPTER NINE

1 What does Victor agree to do?
2 What promise does the creature make?

CHAPTER TEN

1 Why does Victor damage the female creature?
2 What does he do with the female creature's body parts?
3 Why does Victor have to go with the crowd of Irish men?

CHAPTER ELEVEN

1 Who is the man who was murdered on the beach?
2 Which two people come to visit Victor in prison?
3 What important thing happens after Victor returns to Geneva?

CHAPTER TWELVE

1 What does Victor believe that the creature is planning to do?
2 What does the creature actually do?

CHAPTER THIRTEEN

1 Where does Victor go to "speak" to William, Elizabeth and his father?
2 What promise does Victor make to his family?
3 Five people have died because of the creature. Who are they?

CHAPTER FOURTEEN

1 What does Robert Walton think about Victor Frankenstein's story?
2 What do you think happens to the creature after the end of the story?
3 What do you think Robert Walton does after the end of the story?

After-reading questions

1 Does your opinion of the creature change during the story?
2 The creature calls Victor a "miserable, selfish man". Do you agree with this description? Why/Why not?
3 Does Victor do the right thing when he decides to break his promise and damage the female creature, do you think?
4 The book was written at a time of many important scientific discoveries. Mary Shelley uses those ideas, and the fear they created, in her story. What scientific discoveries and fears might she use if she were writing the story today?

Exercises

1 **Choose the correct modal verb to complete these sentences in your notebook.**

1 "I am following someone, and I *must* / **can** continue my search."

2 I was very, very happy. Why did those days **must / have to** end?

3 My parents decided that I **have to / should** study science at Ingolstadt University.

4 "I have always thought that in the future you **had to / should** marry."

5 "You **mustn't / haven't to** worry about me − I have had a full and happy life."

6 We were all shocked and upset, but life **must to / had to** continue.

2 **Complete the sentences in your notebook, using the words or phrases from the box.**

> when   experiments   scientist   laboratory   then
> after   monster   from that day forward

¹ ...*When*... he arrived at university, Victor met an amazing and interesting ²............ called Professor Waldman. ³............, Victor thought only about science and studying. He spent hours doing his own ⁴............ in a ⁵............ in his own apartment. ⁶............ one day he discovered how to create life itself! He decided to make a man, but, ⁷............ the creature came to life, Victor saw that he had made a ⁸.............

CHAPTER FIVE

3 **Write the correct noun in your notebook.**

	adjective	*noun*
1	happy	*happiness*
2	dead	....
3	sad	....
4	dark	....
5	shocked	....
6	dangerous	....
7	guilty	....
8	foggy	....

CHAPTERS SIX AND SEVEN

4 **Put the sentences in the correct order in your notebook.**

a .... I lived very simply in the forest, learning about myself and my body.

b .... I spent the next days and weeks studying the books and teaching myself to read.

c .... Soon everyone in the village was outside, shouting and running after me.

d .... Later that day I found a very small wooden hut that was next to a small cottage.

e ....1.... I started to move, and I discovered that I could walk.

f .... I lived this way for a long time, watching the family and learning about their lives.

g .... I walked and walked for hours, until I came to the forest at Ingolstadt.

h .... I was exploring deep in the forest one night when I found a bag with books inside it.

CHAPTER EIGHT

5 **Write these statements as reported speech in your notebook.**

1 "I'm a traveller who needs some rest," the creature told the old man.

The creature told the old man that he was a traveller who ....
needed some rest ....

2 The old man said, "That is very sad. I'm sure you will find friends."

3 "I'm a very good person," the creature said.

4 "Their view will change," the old man told the creature.

5 "My father is Mr Frankenstein, and he'll come and find you!" the boy shouted at the creature.

6 "Then you belong to my enemy, and I'm going to kill you!" the monster told the boy.

6 **Put these words into two groups in your notebook.**

confused	upset	loving	worried	miserable
	shocked	exciting	pleased	

Positive meaning	Negative meaning
	confused

7 **Complete these sentences in your notebook, using** *will* **or** *would.*

1 I did not know what this female creature ...*would*.. be like.

2 If she wanted to kill people, it .... be very difficult to stop her.

3 If I decided wrongly, perhaps many more bad things .... happen.

4 "I .... never again make another creature. I cannot!"

5 "I .... not change my mind. Go! Leave me alone!"

6 "Remember this – I .... be with you on your wedding night."

CHAPTER ELEVEN

8 **Write the correct verb, active or passive, in your notebook.**

1 I *was taken* / **took** to a large, important-looking building in the centre of the town.

2 "The boat **was being sailed** / **was sailing** away from the beach by one man."

3 "I think it was the same boat that I **was seen** / **saw** this man arrive in."

4 "I'm sorry that you **are being kept** / **are keeping** in this awful prison."

5 "In your papers, I also **was found** / **found** a letter from your father."

6 A month later, I **was called** / **called** to go to court.

9 **Write questions for these answers in your notebook.**

1 *Where did Victor and Elizabeth go for a walk before dinner?*
   Along the shore of the lake.

2 He told her to go to their room so that she did not see his fight with the monster.

3 He ran away from the inn towards the lake.

4 He said that he could not help Victor.

5 Until he found the monster and killed him, or until he died.

6 He asked him to kill the creature.

10 **Are these sentences *true* or *false*? Write the correct answers in your notebook.**

1 Robert Walton does not believe Victor's story. *false*

2 Robert Walton thinks Victor may die on the ship.

3 The creature kills his creator, Victor Frankenstein.

4 Robert Walton tries to kill the creature.

5 The creature is planning to kill himself.

An answer key for all questions and exercises can be found at
www.penguinreaders.co.uk

Project work

1 Imagine that Victor chose to stay and calmly talk to the creature instead of running away when his creation first came to life. Write this conversation as a play script.

2 Choose one or more of the murders in the story, and write a newspaper report.

3 Imagine you are Elizabeth on the day she marries Victor, just minutes before she dies. Write a diary page for this day.

4 Compare this book to any films you have seen of *Frankenstein*. How are they the same? How are they different? Why did the writer make these changes to the film, do you think?

5 In this book, the creature is often escaping or hiding. Make a "wanted" poster for the creature. Include a full description, the reasons why he is wanted, and information on how he may behave.

6 The creature says, "I was good and pure, but being alone and hated has made me unhappy and dangerous." How far do you agree that we are all born "good and pure" and that our experiences in life make us who we are? What part does choice play?

7 Write a different ending to the story.

Glossary

bury (v.)
to put a dead body under the ground

carriage (n.)
A *carriage* has four wheels. People sit in it, and it is pulled by horses.

cave (n.)
a large hole in the side of a mountain. People used to live in *caves*.

chase (v. and n.)
If you *chase* someone or something, you follow them and try to catch them. A *chase* is when you follow someone or something and try to catch them.

cottage (n.)
a small house in the countryside (= an area that is not a town or city)

court (n.)
a place where people decide if a person will go to prison

create (v.); **creation** (n.)
To *create* is to make something new. A *creation* is something or someone new that has been made. *Creation* is when something is being made.

creature (n.)
a living person or animal. Sometimes they have been *created*.

depressed (adj.);
depression (n.)
If you are *depressed*, you feel very sad for a long time. *Depression* is a sad feeling that you have for a long time.

discovery (n.)
a piece of information that you discover for the first time

electricity (n.)
Electricity makes machines work. It makes heat and light.

experiment (n.)
You do an *experiment* because you want to see what will happen, or what is true.

faint (v.)
to fall to the ground suddenly. People sometimes *faint* because they are frightened, ill, too hot or have had a very big surprise.

female (n. and adj.)
A *female* is a woman or girl. A person, animal or plant can be *female*.

flash (n.)
a sudden bright light

give up (phr. v.)
to stop doing something

hang (v.)
in this story, to kill someone by
putting something around their
neck and holding them above
the ground

horrific (adj.)
extremely bad

hut (n.)
a small building with one room.
A *hut* is usually made of wood.

inn (n.)
a small hotel in the countryside
(= an area that is not a town
or city)

innocent (adj.)
If you are *innocent*, you did
not do something bad.

laboratory (n.)
a room where *scientists* do
experiments

lightning (n.)
a sudden bright light that you
see in the sky when there is
a storm

magistrate (n.)
an important person who listens
to information about a crime
and decides if someone is guilty

mind (n.)
Your *mind* is the part of your
body that you use to think and
understand things. If you change
your *mind*, you change what you
think about something.

miserable (adj.)
very unhappy

mixture (n.)
when you put two or more
different things together

monster (n.)
in stories, a very big and
frightening person or animal

nightmare (n.)
a bad dream

phrase (n.)
a group of words that mean
something

power (n.)
in this story, a special ability
to do something

professor (n.)
an important teacher at a
university

rage (n.)
a very strong feeling of anger

refuse (v.)
to say no to doing something

regret (n. and v.)
Regret is when you feel sad
because you did something, or
did not do something.

revenge (n.)
You get *revenge* on someone when
you do something to hurt them
because they did something to
hurt you.

right (n.)
If something is your *right*, you
should be allowed to do it.

sailor (n.)
someone who works on a ship

scared (adj.)
frightened or worried

scientific (adj.); **scientist** (n.)
Scientific things are things
that are used to do *experiments*.
A *scientist* is someone who
does *experiments*.

shore (n.)
the land at the edge of a sea or
lake (= an area of water)

sledge (n.)
You sit on a *sledge* to travel across
snow or ice. *Sledges* are often
pulled by dogs.

suffer (v.)
If you *suffer*, you feel bad.
For example, you might feel
unhappy, ill, too cold, have
pain, etc.

survive (v.)
to stay alive when life is hard
or dangerous

terrified (adj.)
very frightened

upset (adj.)
sad or worried about something
that has happened

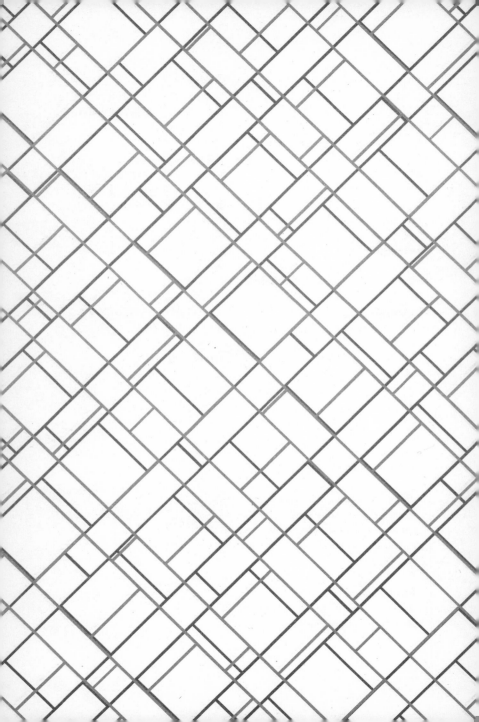